FROM:

TO: ReBBecca.

With LoVE
06-17-2016.

JUSTICE, PEACE, AND LOVE

JUSTICE, PEACE, AND LOVE

FOR ESPAÑA LA COLOMBIANA

ESPAÑA COLES

To order additional copies of this book, contact:
Xlibris Corporation
1-888-795-4274
www.Xlibris.com
Orders@Xlibris.com
39567

Contents

Acknowledgements

Thank you to all my friends,

My loved ones,

To my loving family

And all those who are dear to me.

Mr. President Albaro Uribe

Good, bad if you're liked, or not, you have to live with that
Working from early morning to dark
Eight dollars a day, two hundred and fifteen dollars a month, and two
thousand five hundred and eighty dollars a year, who cares, this is the
bulgar minimum wage, and this is it if you are lucky to find a job
or the other way, go to hell
Can a family live with that pay and have a decent life?
To pay rent, education, transportation, doctors, clothes,
and everything else
To live like this embarrasses me because this is not enough
I think who is doing this is not using his mind; nobody can support
a family with that
Believe it or not, this is treating the people like slaves
Do you have children and a wife?
Can they survive with that little and *bulgar* minimum wage?
Can you think about how the poor people live?
When they have to be very, very tight or have just bananas and rice
They have to change their life going to *tirofijo* side
They sacrifice their life trying to keep their family alive

A Little Bit or a Lot

Stand on your feet and think about yourself
Think about your value and what a nice person you are
Figure out if your love deserves you
Now tell me the truth, is that good?
Did he love you a lot or just a little bit?
Do you deserve that, or do you just want to live with that?
Do you want to be happy, or do you want to beg for love?
Think about love, it's everywhere in the world
And do not throw your life away because love is not something that you
can make grow with when it is not by your side and in your heart
It is sad to live with an illusion that time will change the love
And somebody will love you more then than now
Please figure this out

American President

Colombians, Mexicans, Central Americans, Venezuelans, Cubans,
and Brazilians
We are here for the same dream
Listen, Mr. President, we are not delinquents; we are not fugitives
We come to this country to plant and pick your crops with our hands
In winter or in summer, they would be food for the worms
Please stop treating us like pigs
When we are working hard from the morning to the night in the
cold or the heat
Many look at us like a pig, waiting to eat for free
We are people; we are running away from our countries
Because we want to be alive and don't want to see our family die by our
side like a parasite
We are taking care of the country to keep the economy up and to keep
our country and our family in a decent life
We want respect from you because we are showing you that with our job
Always remember that we know where we were born but will never
know where we will die.
God made the land, and he never said that this land was not for us
We are peaceful people who put our life in danger to come here to work
No more discrimination
No more persecution
Let us work, and give us love

February 17, 1996

On February 17 at the Bonilla Aragon
At four in the afternoon, I got on the airplane
When I put on my seat belt, I left one part of my heart
From that day on, I spend remembering you
My beautiful nation
I only see you on television and ask God to stop the corruption
I am writing a petition to the boss of the nation
Mr. President Misael Pastrana
To give everybody a job
And you will see that with this, the killing will stop
When everybody can turn the stoves on
Because an empty stomach damages the heart and the mind
Nobody thinks bad with a full stomach
This was what I was living there
When there, Mauricio Guzman Cali Estava was directing
He took me out from a place where I was selling fruit
Because the city was putting up metal statues of the poets
That was more important to the government
Than families with children
When that happened, my fruit were rotting
And my children were getting dangerously close to malnutrition
It wasn't Mr. President's fault
Because he wasn't president by that time
I remember that he was competing with Mr. Samper Pizano
And Samper won the election, and at that moment he started giving
orders, and from el Cam, the Mayor Mauricio Guzman was following
them, and started running away all the poor people that were
working at the street
I'm not giving any congratulations to President Pastrana

I'm only verifying
Because four years later when you won the election, you start
attacking the honest and poor working people
And the delinquents and some policemen
Were free and stealing together
I was filling hate in my heart because sometimes
I didn't have to start the stove
This was one of the reasons I had to leave my beautiful country
I was sitting down on a chair resting at the Paseo Bolivar after a
peaceful protest to ask President Samper Pizano to give us a solution
to work to feed our family
When the Virgin Mary was revealed to me
I met my husband, a man from another country
She gave me my husband, my angel of salvation
I love you, my husband
I love you, Colombia
I love you, Oregon
This is the time to change the nation, Mr. President
And you will see the change in people's hearts
And you could be seen as a hero to the new generation
The fire wasn't even able to take your name
And now I am going to my bed, and I will wake up tomorrow to listen to
the good news from my land, I would like to hear that all the news is to
change the country and the land
The shouting Colombian lady wouldn't have reason to write this song

Angry River

I did not pass the river Bravo, and I do not want to imagine
But if you pass this, please do not forget this experience
And all the time, remember to pass this and to step on American soil,
you have to get wet and maybe dirty the water
Drink and, if you are lucky, win some paper from this country, do
not forget that those are borrowed; and before you open your mouth,
connect your tongue to your brain; never call them illegal and wet
backs. Think about where you come from
And never hurt the feelings of your mother and father's nation
Because you don't have a clue, you are a crazy egg

Another Took Your Place

You left me with my heart broken
I waited for you for many years, and you never came back
like you promised me
You went to the USA to look for fortune, but you found an American
lady there who spoke English to your ears, and you forgot what
you promised me
The years passed by and I healed my broken heart
Today you came back to tell me you were very sorry and you had
money, but no love
I had to tell you sorry back because another had already took your place
When you knocked on the door, my husband answered
When you asked him for my name, you were surprised because my
husband told you that I was his wife and you had lost me
What did you think, that love is occasional and is something you can
leave and pick back up when you return?
Love is spread everywhere because it is all around us
To find a good love is a gift from God

Are You at Life?

Some men call women weak or feeble, but this is a big mistake
We are stronger than everything; we are the only people who can bear
children and produce life
We can keep another person for nine months in our body
more than one time
Those who call us weak or feeble are very far away from life
Because he doesn't have a clue how he came to life
If you feel that you are alive, turn back, think about it, and always
remember, before you hurt a woman, you are hurting your mom

Memories

I can't forget you
Your memory follows me
I love you like nobody, and you pay me poorly
But today I promise to forgive you
Today I throw your memories to the ocean
To keep them there
Because here on land, you can damage another one
The kisses that you gave me I erased them too with the kisses from
another man who knows how to love me
From this moment, you are out of my life
There at the ocean your memories found a place
To stop making other women cry like you did to me

Brother Sebastian

Brother, you who live and did not say good-bye
We are waiting for an answer from you every day
And looking for you from when the sun rises till it sets
When you left without saying anything to your children and
their mother
Your children have already grown up and became men and women
Your grandchildren are asking for their grandfather
But there is no answer
You left a pain in our hearts
I have a feeling that you are alive, but sometimes I lose hope
Please send proof that you are alive, wherever you are
We are waiting for your return
With love and wish you are coming back
Your sisters España, Dilia, Eduicia, Flor, and Sorlenny
Your brothers Camilo, Calisto, Pedro Juan, and Asimeon
Your children's mother Sara
Your children Sebastian, Miller, and Gustavo, who is already in the sky
because somebody took his life away
And your grandchildren
We love you, brother

Brother Pedro Juan

He who left many years ago to Venezuela telling your only son and
his mother that you were coming back because you got tired of the
sugarcane job and you were looking for a better life
I remember that you made a couple of trips with our brother Calisto,
and you came back home
But from trip number 3 or 4, our brother came back by himself
He said that he told you that he was coming home, and you only said to
say hello to your son and his mother
When you left, your son was a little boy and time started passing, and he
turned into a handsome man
He was a good son, taking care of his mother
He got married and had three children who don't know their grandfather
The time was not enough for your son to keep waiting for you because
God called him to the sky in a tragic accident
He was riding his motorcycle, and a taxicab crashed into him
and killed him
Leaving behind his children, his wife, his mother, and a father that
doesn't know that he is already in the sky
If you are alive, please send proof to your grandchildren and us
If you are in the sky, find your son and ask him to forgive you and tell
him the reason why you left him
We miss you, brother Pedro Juan, and want to know something about
you. Your grandchildren.
Your sisters España, Flor, Sorlenny, Eduicia, and Dilia
Your brothers Camilo, Calisto, Asimeon, and Sebastian, who
disappeared one morning after you left and never came back
The same way you did
We love you wherever you are, and you are in our hearts

Children Services

Money or love keeps your children away from the state
This is not something that you want to live
Some of the people are good and work for love
But many of them just do damage to you and your family's life
Because many of them grew up in the state's care, and they are
trying to avenge
If you can keep your children away from the state, do it because they
can smell anything to put your children away for a long time
for no reason
The state is a troublemaker because when the children are in a
dangerous situation, the state could be next door, and they won't
do anything about it
They wait until the children are already dead

Delinquent Cigarette

It feels hot and smells bad
This is a war crossing all the continent
From the Oriental to the Occident
Please be present, Mr. President
Because the cigarette is a delinquent
It is contaminating and killing the people
Here dies the guilty and the innocent
I want you to tell me who is the law
This is an emergency
Because you were intelligent, you are the president
And you have the power to stop this war
When I was little, I was listening
They were closing the *tabacaleras*
But everything was a lie
Because today we have cigarette contraband
You listen to commercials on all the channels
Inviting the people to try the most expensive
The patriotic symbols are sacred
And we have to respect them
But today when I went to the store
I have a terrible impression
When I was looking for matches
I saw the US flag shining in a cigarette carton
I ask you, Mr. President, start an investigation
And remove the flag from the carton
Because the patriotic symbols, they are part of our hearts
Do not let anybody step on tradition

Colombian American

For my native Colombian land and America, my second land,
I would give my life for your liberty
Because both of you are part of my life
Thank you, my native land, for giving me the vision to teach me
how to fight with just my heart
Thank you, my second land, for keeping me out of a bad life and for
giving me an opportunity for my children and me to have a decent life
I promise I will never forget what you have given me
I was not born here, but I love you with all my heart
If you ever need me, I will be here to defend you from the bad hands
that want to backstab us
Because whoever damages you damages my life too
I ask God to turn his eyes down to the land and change all the bad hearts
in the world and bring us peace

Where Are Our Colombian Human Rights?

I just see what we have here is rights to the worms
If we do not shut our mouth when we see a crime and the corruption
Now, everybody, when they are bad, they are free to do what they want
because they do not have justice
The corruption starts there
We have eyes to see but no mouth to talk
All Colombians, get up and fight for your human rights
For peace and your life
Fight for your family's life, defend yourself
No more crime and no more Colombians dead
Nobody is going to take care of you or your family
We cannot do anything to defend our family, just to wait for the enemy
to take us and our family's life out
If somebody hits you, hit them back and violence will stop
This is time for the president and the law to let the good people to take
care of their own lives
Because there is no reason to die with our hands tied behind our back
And die like a parasite or see your family killed
Defend your life wherever you go, be prepared
Do not let someone take your life

Columbia River

The Columbia River starts its life in Canada
And spraying two states, Washington and Oregon
Passing by Biggs Junction, you steal my heart
When I see your sweet water moving with frenzy
You take me back to the place I was born
Every moment during the day, I can't stop looking at you
From dawn to dusk
You are part of my life
It does not matter if I go away; you will be with me forever

Crazy Law

Oh my goodness, what is that?
A crazy law by changing the law
Telling the parents not to spank their kids before they turn four
If you don't listen and you spank your kids
The jail will be open for one year, or you can pay the
one-thousand-dollar fine.
Oh my goodness, this is something very bad; help this crazy lady and
send her to the mental hospital to mind better
Can you think about what a parent has to do when a little child gets out
of control, throwing themselves everywhere, and you can't spank them?
Or when your child runs out in the street and throws itself down
in traffic?
I am a lady, but when I see a lady acting that way, it makes me
embarrassed to be a lady.
I believe that women are so smart, and we can do anything we set
our minds to.
But ladies like her need to be away from a powerful position

Crazy Man

I think that you have changed, but you are still the same
You are going into the world, destroying the feelings of the lady
And throwing children like a bird when lost from the nest
Your blood and your last name don't have any value to you
The time never stops, but you have not thought about your children
and how you treat them like lost eggs
I am watching this, so be careful because if you don't stop Deceiving
your lady and ignoring the existence of your children
When you're old, you will be sad, and you will be abandoned like
a dog on the street

Cut of Love

They swore their love until they die
Promise that time took away
Like the wind that leaves the trees that the fall withered
He was very hardworking, honest, and dedicated to his children
and his wife
But one day, he forgot that love is like the flowers that are in winter and
in the summer if we do not get the attention that they need
One day she made a mistake, and from that day her marriage
was finished
They tried to be together until the fruit of their love flowered
But the time was like an enemy, and every day, the cut was growing
He could not bear the pain because the cut was so deep that it
would not heal

My Sister Dilia's Poem

When I remember my land, I feel happiness
Because this was where I spent the best years of my life
Land beautiful and lovely, where I was born at the faraway land at the
municipality of Sipi, there with my three sisters
When my mother died, my father and my stepmother, with a lot of love,
took care of us until the day they died
Today they already are in the sky together with my mother
It doesn't matter the distance because I can feel their eyes looking
everywhere I walk

Dirty and Shoeless

Dirty and shoeless old people and children in the cold streets
of the capital
They walk day and night.
Out of hope to find a home
Looking in the garbage for a piece of bread
It does not matter if it is rotten
The government knows this necessity, but they make themselves blind
and ignore the problem
While the rich ride in their limousines, eating exquisite foods
They lost hope of life with the indifference and the look of people
looking at them like a piece of garbage
The governors do not do anything to give a solution to these problems
that every day is growing like wheat
Sometimes I think the rich are happy with the suffering of the
poor people
Crazy government, please put love in your foot on the floor
To bring peace to our country Colombia.
The cure for this is feeding the hungry!
This is a reality, stop spending money.
This money can be spent on food to feed hungry people.
Not spending it on them is like buying a weapon to kill them.
The solution is killing the hunger
Think about what you would do if you see your mother, your father,
your wife, or your children crying in pain because they are so hungry,
and there is nothing to eat.
Give me an answer; will you sit in front of them and watch them die
alongside you like a coward?
Tell me that you won't do something criminal if you did not have a job
or help from the government to feed your family
To keep them alive.

Drugs Are Death

Do not do drugs; they are death
Do not know the people that are selling them
They are a war; they are the destruction
Do not do drugs; they will damage your brain
Do not do drugs; they will damage your family and
everything around them
Drugs are very bad
Put them away, and they are somebody that you can't fight,
don't have any help
Please look for that because the drugs can send your love to hell
I curse drugs; I curse the author
It is a war and a cursed addiction
Who is doing this garbage does not care about anything
They do not care if they kill their own generation

Eating for Free

Presidents from the present and the future, this is the time to use your mind and stop taking the money away from the honest and hardworking people

You feed the lazy people who aren't old or sick; this is like a joke to me and makes me feel like a slave

This is the time to send everyone to work and make money to support themselves

I have been working here for many years now, and I have paid many taxes to feed the lazy people

I have not seen any change; I need this money to feed my family who is having a bad situation

I feel very bad when I see many people from this country and from other countries working hard in the cold and in the heat, and the lazy people are just waiting to eat for free

Mr. President, you can change this and make everybody work and just have their parents feed them

Embarrassed

I feel embarrassed and mad when I read the newspaper from
my country Colombia
This is a nightmare when I see there the discrimination
And the government does not do anything to defend human rights
There, you can read the Help Wanted ads and see they are
discriminating, asking for age and skin color
If you are over thirty, you are too old to find a job
When I see this discrimination, I wish to have magic to remove the
president that is farting in the chair
Ignoring the poor people and their pain; these are the same people that
made him president
I don't believe the politicians when they speak and make promises
because they are rich and they don't know what it's like to be hungry
They only know to acknowledge the poor when they need a vote
Those who are noble and honest
They put them in a coffin before they are elected

Family

Your family is more important than anything
Look at how you treat your family
They give you the same treatment; when you do not have respect for
them, when you do not have respect for your families, you can't have a
good relationship with your husband or his family
Because the respect starts in your house, and you have to do whatever
you need to have good relationship and good treatment
But if you don't look back and see how you value your own parents
The family must have to think that if you don't value your relatives, how
can you value somebody else?
When you respect your parents, everyone respects you
They know that if they do something to you, your parents
will defend you
You must remember always that you loved your parents before you had
your husband's family
Your husband and your kids learned how to love you

The Colombian Flag

When I see the colors yellow, blue, and red
For more strength that I do
My eyes cry forever
They are inevitably strong; I cannot stop
When I remember the flag from my original land
That makes me remember when I was a little girl
There in my *selba chocoana*
In the corner of the Colombian Pacific Coast
Where the only green were wheat and iguanas
And today, for fault of the government,
People now grow marijuana
I ask my Father God to remember the choco
Where the poverty grows the same as nature
Turn your eyes to the land you have created
Because the government is not doing the mission you gave to them

In Memory of *Palomo Uzuriaga*

On the Twenty-eighth Street, he was born
Here he spent his childhood and turned into a man
The same place where a bad hand took his life away
You can see a very sad sister and a destroyed mother
Because one part of her heart is already buried with her son
Who one day gave happiness and made the country shake
when he gave glory to Colombia, kicking hard the football
Only one year after his death, the judge closed the investigation
The fiscal was already tired, leaving the case closed
They made him look like an abandoned dog on the street
And not the son of a mother that in her life lived with him
The same to his family and friends, he left an empty space in their hearts
Their house looks very empty; it doesn't feel happy and no music is played
I am not present, but I can feel that
He inspired happiness to the children with his smile
He was helping children and some people too
I ask the judge to have it presented that he was a son of Colombia
And don't throw him to the shadows
And to the one who took his life, give his family an answer
Why he took that decision, taking Albeiro's life
Without any explanation
Only activating one gun and stopping his heart
At thirty-seven years old, he was just starting his life
One night very early, the neighborhood was crying for him
The same faraway watching the television
When they said his name, my heart was pounding
And my eyes cried, and my hands were shaking
Because of another Colombian whose life somebody took away
When I was thinking of his mother and the pain that she was feeling
Like a little girl with no defense
Tears I were spilling

Forever in My Heart

You are in my heart from the moment I saw you; the love was there
with the first look
I was waiting for all my life; I let every offer of love pass because I
know that one day you would come into my life
You sat by my left side five minutes after I sat with you and invited me
to have something to drink
I drank beer to celebrate the start of our love
You returned at the same time days later
When you left, it was so hard to see you going to your country and
say good-bye
I cried a lot, but I knew that you would come back
After you left, I was counting the seconds, minutes, hours, and days
until eight months passed before you came back to pick me up to be
together for the rest of our lives

The Colombian Fruit Seller

I remember at Samper Pizano a Colombian president
This was the one who made me putrefy all my bananas
One morning very early
I started working at the street, selling fruits to support my children
When a policeman intimidated me with a gun on his hip
He told me to leave soon and to never come back
This was an order from the mayor
Made for the president; if you don't listen, you will be finished or jailed;
I remember that moment; it's in my mind forever
Moving the poor and honest workers
But not moving the delinquents
I remember the president's name; I don't have to think very long; all I
have to do is see a banana

The Colombian Girl

I grew up with no shoes on my feet
There in a corner, a Colombiano
Where we only hear the name of the Colombian presidents
The children of my region
grow up without protection of the state
We only receive two things from the Colombiano government infected
shots and some teachers leaving at the year's end
I have an infected shot
When I look at my shoulder, there is a mark
If my father didn't cure me
To not make the history long, my arm had to be cut
Seasons change, anniversaries pass
And I remember, the name of the president was
Belizario

Gold Wasn't for Us

I have a pain in my heart that is difficult to cure
I remember the day I left my two kids to look for gold
I do not remember the date because it hurts me a lot
Only thing I remember was that it was almost dark when I took a bus to
leave; it was like a stake in my heart
I cried through the night; I didn't leave my kids because I wanted to, I
just didn't want to see them crying from not having enough and living
with a lot of necessity
My friend that owns the house that I was renting
invited me to a place where there was a lot of gold, and I took the offer
to go with my friend and her sister, but the gold was not for us; when the
gold is not for you, you can walk on top of it and never see it
We worked from morning to night with a shovel
We moved a lot of mud, but all our prospects were very poor
When we finished the hole, it was very sad for all of us, so we kept
working, and we had to move because we did not find any gold
Just a little to drink and something to eat
Now we started getting sick and going to the doctors one at a time
because when one was getting better the other one was coming
down with it
We did not die, but one of us was close to it, but it was not our time
We had many years to go. The time started passing, and it was difficult
to put money together to come back
We kept working hard, but it was not looking good for us
Some people get rich in just one day
One day my friend decided to come back, and I had to turn her down
and look for another job, and the time passed fast, but money was
not enough

41

Good Job

to my father—and mother-in-law, Dale and Joan

Thank you for giving me your son, and thank you for raising a good
man, and thank you for teaching him what it is to be honest and
what love is
Every time we have a big problem, he tells me, I am going to talk with
my mom and dad to help me and tell me what they do to keep their
marriage together; they never break up
Thank you for teaching my husband what it is to be a real dad
I'm sure that you know that he who is a good son will be a good
husband and a good dad; this is not something you learn in school; it is
taught from Mom and Dad
Thank you for loving your grandkids very much
And thank you, Mom and Dad, for being there to help us out with
everything and for being good to your daughter-in-law
Thank you for your patience and all the love
I love you very much

Do Not Hate The Good Emmigrants

Do not hate us, do not send us back, just send the bad people
We are here looking for protection, love, and jobs
Sometimes in our country, the government won't give us, and we have to
leave everything, our families, and our country
Are you going to do the same to us?
Can you think how this country would be if you send everyone back?
I can tell you that the country would be very poor because there will not
be anymore fruit or vegetables
You'll have to get us and bring us back to work because a lot of people
here don't know how to grow crops, and they don't have a clue
what to do there
You have to understand that land is for everybody who cares about it; do
not forget that you were born here, but your ancestors fought to get this
land, and we do not fight
We just want respect and a better life

Hero of No Compensation

To all soldiers that are in the war
Fighting for my freedom
Composing this *extrofas* today
I could not stop crying
I feel a big pain in my chest
That is crushing my heart
When I see you in front of the battalion
Like a hero doing your missions
You don't care where I come from
My color, my race, or my religion
To save my life in the country
You have to sacrifice many hearts
The hardest part is leaving your family
When you don't know if you are coming back from that region
Walking like you did on that day you left
Or maybe in a coffin
God bless your mother, your father
your children, and your wife for their great sacrifice
And God cover you with blessings
And your image not be forgotten
Like someone that gives everything
And ask nothing in return
To save us from *em boscada*
When was leaving everything back
Wife, father, mother, and children worry
With their hearts beating
Afraid of a bad call when the phone when ringing
They felt the same sensation
When the other continent showing the news
From the channel of the *te lemundo*
That *ana patricia and pedrito* are showing

I Know How to Stop the War

The government from my town, my town of Colombia
The poor people, Indians and black, they treat us like a pig
With miserable pay, sometimes it's not enough to buy rice or bananas
If we are not careful, we will be cleaning our butts with our hands
Because this pay is not enough to eat and buy toilet paper
If we keep spending millions looking for peace
Ignoring that with this hunger, this is never coming back
Please open your eyes, or let a poor person to take care of our country
Take this from somebody that knows what it's like to feel
hungry and cold
If I were the president, I could walk outside without a guard because the
poor people would protect me from the rich
The guerrillas would come back by themselves when they see that
liberty and human rights are coming back with somebody just and
knows what is the necessity of the people

I Love You, Moro

Moro is a little town in Sherman County, Oregon
Where the wheat grows a lot, and it is here where I found my love
I love you, Moro, very much; thank you for giving me my husband
Todd, wherever I go, you are in my heart; I move to another place,
but don't take this like a treachery; I just move where I feel so happy
because it takes me back to my place where
I was born and grew up
I hope that you don't get jealous; I hope that you don't get mad; I will
have you in my heart for the rest of my life, and I will have you too if
one day I die; thank you for growing into a good man

Colombia, My Beautiful Land

Colombia, my beautiful land so amazing and serene
I ask God for your liberation from the human backstabber
I especially ask for the mistake of President Pastrana
Begging of the black lady
I was born of the *Choco* land
Walking on the branches, free like an iguana
And today I am leaving to the American lands
I'm not just doing this dedication to President Pastrana
This is dedicated to all the people that do the branch
I had a pain in my chest; I had to get up from my bed to write this recital
To take something from my heart that was killing me
The name was loneliness
The president's actions are intolerable
They are taking our freedom to walk on our streets and to hug
our ancestors
I want to see my family
I want to go back soon
When I feel sick and down
Only saying your name gives me strength
Today with love and pride from my heart to give you this *estrofas*
Like the leaves falling from a tree when the seasons change
I have something to tell you; do not take this like a stab in the back
To share my heart and my love with another beautiful land
in the state of Oregon
This is the land of my husband, my angel of salvation
But I have something present in my mind and heart
I do not care if delinquent presidents and people try to divide
the country
Forever you will be Colombia
The land that Christobal Colon discovered

47

Thank You to God and My Parents

Every day when I open my eyes
I cannot stop saying thank you to God and my parents
Who gave me life and took care of my family and me
Everything in the universe fills my heart
The sun makes me happy and smile
The rain gives me peace and relaxation
The stars and the moon invite me to live in this land forever
Who doesn't love the life is dead and was never born
Every night when I lay down
I am ready for another morning
The days are short, and the nights are too
Because the life is so beautiful to be enjoyed

Ligia's Grandmother

Olave Mary Cristina
Grandmother Mary Cristina, I'm here in the kitchen
Remembering your season and your chicken soup
Grandmother Mary Cristina, I have you in my heart
Any time I remember you, tears come to my eyes
You will be forever in my mind and my heart
It doesn't matter that you are living in a different world
I'm very sure that you are singing
To the angels, the Virgin, and Father God
Talent that here on the land nobody recognized
Grandmother Mary Cristina, from here today I sing to you
In honor of your memory, your granddaughter has inherited your voice
The songs you were singing, and your voice never was recorded
You were the best voice that the river Naya Borth
In the little town the *concha se oye rezonar tu voz*
Dedicated to my friend Ligia Zamora's Grandmother

Love Is Life

Marriage is half-and-half
Do not try to be the boss; let your husband do the half
Because a marriage like that never works out
Be like a lady and do not treat your husband bad
But don't let your husband treat you bad
Give him love and make him love you back
Remember always that marriage is to have something to share, and love
doesn't run away for a little thing
Do not try to be a man because your children need to know who is mom
and who is dad
And when they grow up, they will do the same that they saw from
Mom and Dad
Learn how to say I am sorry when you are wrong
Do not go to bed mad because you will miss that when one of you
is gone
Men, do not try to be big and bad because you came from
women's body
You are a partner and you are a friend; we are the same
Always show your husband or your wife that they are very important; be
happy, patient, compassionate, and proud that you have somebody that
loves you
This is an agreement that you swore to God to be there through the good
and the bad times
Remember, love is life

When Love Leaves

When you find a real love, you must take care of it
Because if you let it go, it may never come back
Real love is tenderness, patience, and security
Love is there through the good and the bad
Love does not care if you are sick or poor
Real love never leaves you
Do not hurt this with a lie or treachery
Because love never forgets
This is not a mistake; it will kill the feeling forever
Because there is nothing in the world that can cure this cut

Love Found and Love Lost

to my friend

One afternoon in the summer
I was walking on the warm sand next to the river Naya
I met a love, but the years passed
I had to leave to work to pay for my school because my family did not
have any money
He went to another city too, but we had many dreams of coming back to
get married, but destiny crossed our way
A bad hand took his life away, breaking my heart, leaving me lonely
for years
This pain stayed with me for many years
I left everything to God to do his verdict

When Love Puts You Down

Do not live with somebody who does not know what love is
Because a real love never puts you down, hurting your feelings, and
does not make you feel lost
When somebody loves you, for real, they do not make you cry and they
give you security
It does not matter if there is money or not
If you are living in this condition, please wake up
Look for a door to live another life because life is too short
To know this kind of love is like living in a prison
Love is liberty, and you do not have to be sad
If you have love, you can find a way to live free and not to live like dead

Love Song

I sing to the love; I sing to the life
When I leave, I sing and I sing when I am back
I love to sing because life is so beautiful, and the music keeps me up
together with my family and together with my friends
I say leave the life; I say leave the love
The war should die and leave the peace
And everybody laugh during the day and during the night
And leave respect for all the good people
And nobody tries to take another person's life
No more parents crying for their children because
an abusive person took their life because of a misunderstanding
Leaving sadness and an empty house

Love Yourself

Before you love somebody, learn to love yourself
Love is beautiful, and it is good to love
But before you love somebody, you need to learn to love yourself
If you do not love yourself, you can't love somebody
Love yourself and teach your love to love you
Love everything that you have because life is beautiful but too short
Do not let one minute pass; be happy just to be alive
Be happy wherever you are because nothing can change you
It doesn't matter if yourself with makeup
Or if you have a surgery, it won't change your brain or your heart
Feel proud of who you are
Who doesn't feel happy to be alive and healthy?
Those that spend their time being mad are already dead

The Love's End

I did not know the reason when I lost you
With your departure, you left my heart destroyed
You killed my dreams and my illusions in only one moment
I was looking at the door with a wish you were coming back
I was looking everywhere we were walking
I cannot forget the afternoon when I saw you kissing her
You were taking her hand, and you did not care that I was there
Like two adolescents, from that day, I promised myself
That I was not throwing one more tear for you
Today I find a love that loves me and will show me real love

Marlyn on Her 19th

Marlyn turned nineteen, and in September, she is moving
She is not moving to our country of Colombia
She is staying in Oregon where she can get an education
I am not talking bad about my country's education
But if you don't have money or good luck
You will live an illusion, and you won't have profession
Only in your imagination
Because at the university you won't get through the door
When she was in high school, she told her mother every day that she
was leaving to her nation the day after she graduates
Her grandparents offered her a ticket for the airplane
But she changed her mind, and she took the money for the ticket and
invested in a computer instead

Marriage Is for Two

Communication is important
A marriage without communication is like a garden without flowers
A marriage is for two people, not just for one
When the communication dies, it is the same when the river dries up;
it is very sad to see a river dry because the people have to leave to find
water somewhere else
The same goes for a marriage because when it dries up, one of them
leaves, looking for another love or without it
Never keep secrets from your husband or your wife
Tell them your dreams or your thoughts
Show them your emotions when you are happy or sad
Make your life easy and make her or him happy with a little bit of it.

Mary the Teacher

Mary is a teacher that works at the school
She is my accuser
Because of this woman, I had to go to the doctor
My blood pressure was going up and down every moment
If something happened to me, she would have to give an answer
to my family
Now my name was at the court and on the computer too
And when I go to the street, the people that do not know me
tell rumors that are not true
Tell me, teacher, tell me what I am going to do now
You have a tong like a rope
Why don't you take care of your own son?
He is selling drugs and making them right under your nose
Mrs. Teacher, where is the defender
The lady who accused me today?
Because I spanked my son for taking a calculator
Look what you have done to me; I'm destroyed and crying every
moment for three years
And your child is killing children with his drugs
Hear, I have a question and I hope you can give me an answer
I am sure that I don't have to act to get my revenge
on everything that you did to me
If you don't stop creating problems for other people and don't start
worrying about your own children, it may be too late for them

Mother

Mother who is in the sky, I am going to wish you a congratulation
It doesn't matter that you are not on the land
You can hear me from the sky
And send me your blessing like you have been doing since
God called you
We were five girls and five boys, and I was nine months old when
you left
And when I started growing, I have kept you in my heart
When I was a little girl, I was looking at the sky
And when I saw a little cloud shaped in a figure
I was thinking that was you, and in my real life I was believing that
was you, Mama

To Mr. President Bush

To you, Mr. President, boss of this nation
To you, Mr. President, I am asking your cooperation
A mother from Colombia wrote you from Oregon
Almost ready to go to prison because I spanked my son with a belt
to keep him out of trouble
I did not want him to end up in prison in the future
The state workers took me to court and didn't give me any attention
They only listened to my son's version and gave him protection
Today he of the state they call him an abused child
They took him from my home
They were threatening me with my two little ones
I can only touch them to give them love
If I discipline them, they will take them away from me
I do not understand the law in this nation
Mr. President, give me an explanation
What's happening here is not happening in my country
Take a look here at your schools, there are many killings
Children killing children and teachers for cries of attention
They kill for bad grades
I hope, Mr. President, from your mansion, you don't do to me
What the judges from Oregon did
I am sending you a message in this song
To untie our hands and let the parents
Discipline their children
And you will see that crime will stop
When I was writing this song
What I saw on television destroyed my heart
Two students killed a retarded boy living on the streets
for entertainment, after being suspended from school

My Chocoan Land

There in my Chocoan land in my nation of Colombia
I want to say hello to all the good people
I am going to start at the river Sipi where I was born
I grew up there with my sisters; all my *poblacion* is in my heart
I am going to take a walk from the start of the river
I say hello to the people from the Marqueza
These people have a lot of integrity there; I stop to have a beer
Later I am going to *teatino*, a land where they make wine
Here I have breakfast and see my late uncle Bruno
Somebody offered me a cigarette but I said no, thank you,
I do not smoke
Do not be mad, my neighbors, I am going to say hello to everybody
Oh, Santa Barbara, this black lady never forget you, but I have to keep
going to the point I love most
The older people die and the young people give this little river its name,
Brazo Nuevo
The river gets dry, and everyone had to leave
I am crying, remembering the day when I lived there with my father.
I loved him a lot, and he took good care of me
He would go to the river and clean every day after my mother died
Another tear comes to my eyes when I remember a special person, my
stepmother Petrona; she was a very good person
She now lives in another zone, the same zone as my mother and father
Now I'm leaving my Brazo Nuevo
The river of my grandparents, uncles, aunts, and cousins; here is where
we were born and lived
Now I am going to pass the little town of playita in the guayabas; I have
an aunt on my mother's side that lives here

My lover Canaveral here is nothing to see just my school
I can never forget you, my little school Santa Terecita
Mr. Alejo is not here; he lives with Mrs. Eleuteria
I do not know how people grind sugarcane
The Murillito left to look for adventure in another place
At the coast where there is a lot at Langost named Buena Ventura with
their hands on their hips, everyone ask why is España not coming here
Do not worry, my people, I am hanging out with everyone
Now I visit the hill at Canaveral; my family and neighbors are happy to
see me because they love me a lot
Here I have cousins, and my departure is from my cousin Jose Dimar;
now I'm passing to another place, Andagollita
It is almost dark; and the people from Sanagustin are getting frustrated;
oh, my lovely Sanagustin home; you are venerable
I have your name embedded on a paper; here is the Liro church where
I got baptized

My Parents

My father and my mother they are in my mind
They are living in a different world
I have memories of my loving father raising me
I have pain for my mother; she died when I was nine months old
The years pass, and I miss them more and more
If you still have your parents, please don't harm them
Because when they leave, you will be very sorry
If you didn't take the time to give them love or treat them good
When they were present
There are some children that act like delinquents
Giving them a bad time and damaging their minds
I am sorry, my friend, if you are one of them
The line is over period

My Mother

to my nephew, Alexander's mother,
my sister Flor Maria

There is a flower in my house that shines in my life
It doesn't matter if the light is not on; she is my loving mother
She is florescent in the winter or in the summer
To give me her hand if I am sick or healthy
She is shiny like the moon, and she has no fortune
More beautiful than a goddess and doesn't have a crown
She has the name of a flower, a good representation
Every day in my life, I give thanks to God and to my grandparents that
sent that beautiful woman that gave me birth.

Open the Door

Love is only what I have here in my chest
I'm yours with only one condition
I promise to love you until I die
Never pain me with betrayal if one day you get tired and stop
loving me
Please take your suitcase and cross the door because if you think that
you will play with me, you are wrong
That will be a big mistake
I am a woman that when I love, I give everything; I swear to you
I do not support treachery
I think that love is so beautiful, and when you love somebody you can't
share that love with someone else
It is not true that love gets confused
It does not matter if you are in the dark
The smell of love is in your mind and in your heart
Do not tell me a lie that you did not see; I won't believe you

Before a Rich Man Died

I was working in a town where there were many gold mines
My job was selling food on the street at a little stand by other venders
One night during the week, a jeep stopped by
The passenger came down and told me hello.
He asked me my name. He asked me if I was married. I said no.
The driver was still in the car; the man ordered fish and told me how
beautiful a woman I was. I like you, and I have been watching you since
I have been in town.
I really like the hardworking ladies like you. Can you go out with me
tonight after you close?
I said no, I cannot go out with you. He asked what time do you close.
I said I do not know.
He took the food to his friend, and they ate a lot.
He was wearing a hat, jeans, and work shirt like a normal worker
from the mine
They had many soda containers in their car.
I figured out there was a lot of people gathering around my stand and
looking at me to see what was going on; this was not normal.
I saw him in magazines before, but I did not recognize that I was talking
to Pablo Escobar
He had a beard and mustache.
But because he looked different, I did not recognize him.
The whole time he was there talking to me, people were walking around
and looking at the tables next to me.
My friend was selling next door, and she was smiling at me because she
knew what was going on.
She knew who he was and so did the other people.
He told me that he was leaving, and he was coming back to pick me up
after I closed. I kept telling him no because I don't date people
I don't know.

67

He paid me, left the change, and said thank you, and that he would be back. After he left, my friend asked me what he was saying to me, and I told her that he was asking me to go out with him and told me he was coming back later to pick me up.

After he left, he drove around town, making a few stops and then he came back to see if was ready to go.

I told him no, I cannot go out with you.

Then he left again, made his last stop, and came back again to say good-bye.

After the people made sure that he had left, my friend and everyone else started coming to my table telling me that I let a good opportunity pass because that was Pablo Escobar and asked if I knew that.

I was surprised to know this, but I did not care

I was famous around there for a while

But the law never asked me anything, but I am sure that they heard the rumors, and they never came

Because it was a town full of gossip

The next day, people said that he spent the night outside of the club and left town very early in the morning

That night I came home and looked at a magazine, it had pictures of him in it, and it was the same man that was inviting me out.

Respect and Love Your Parents

If your parents are alive, take care of them better than a treasure
Because the pain from losing them, there is no compensation
You can live with this if you know how to love them
But if you are different, you will be sorry
There are some kids that treat their parents bad
Like a zero to the left
Until they lose them, they do not know what they lost
They cry like the rain and can refresh the pain

My River Sipi

Beautiful River Sipi with your crystal water
Close to your start doing the corner
With Istmina
Beautiful River Sipi, I have you in my heart
Every time I remember you, tears come to my eyes
I remember when I was a girl in your crystal water
With my sisters and cousins
We were like sardines swimming
The years are passing, and my hair is changing
And there is not one day in my life that I do not remember you
From one corner in Oregon, I feel a big sensation
The sensation you inspire is walking in my body
I have not experienced this in the best swimming pools

Shout of de Colombian Lady

Shout of the Colombian lady living in a faraway land
For fault of the presidents doing their job in pajamas
And putting on their pants when another country calls
They give the wrong version when they know that
We have a lot of corruption in our country
If you walk on some streets, you can see a lot of desolation
Looks and lost eyes looking at the garbage cans
To stop a desire that is like an itching
For its name is hunger that gives us a body cramp
Like the bees when somebody takes their nest
This is an animal instinct, what more, you can't expect
From somebody that knows how to talk with rationality at the same time
But when the father is looking for a job, all the doors are closed
And the family is at the house with a wish
That when he comes back, he will bring something to eat
But what discouragement when the door is open
And he who has the pants comes in with tears in his eyes
And throw himself on a chair, and his mind is ready
To go to the guerillas and rebel against the government

Son at War

Son who is at war fighting for our freedom
I don't stop praying to defend our country and for our return
Because from the day you left, my heart has been there too
I ask God and the Virgin Mary every day to come and clean the stains
from the blood that we have everywhere on the land
And bring with them intelligence to transmit to the men that are
running for president
And to teach them that if they kill the hunger, it will end the
wars everywhere

American Teachers

to Rosa Elarbach

Thank you for giving me your hand
To put together this American dream
I come to congratulate all the teachers
For the big job
Like second parents, they took my hands
Like your brother
They do it with their heart
They did not discriminate against my nationality or my religion
When I came to Oregon
I was like a little baby crying for a bottle that doesn't know
how to speak
They inspire us with their compassion
Sometimes teachers are speaking and teaching their lessons
And some students don't give their attention
And don't respect their rights
Because they give you all their inelegance to teach many people
To me you are the first and the president is second
Because you are present all the time
To give us your hands in winter or summer
Because to be a president you pass through your hands
Thank you to my English teachers from Columbia Gorge
Community College

The Birds' Nest

The birds abandoned their nest to learn to fly
We have in our consciousness when our children grow up
They also will leave like we did to create them
Abandoning our parents, this is like a chain that never ends
Because if we keep them with us and don't let them go
When we leave, they will be lonely
They won't have children and nephews
like a prisoner finishing her family and the generation

The Caseworker

They call him a specialist for family analysis
But who ran this election never had a clue
To interview him for this position
This man came to my house and showed me some papers
to do an interview
He asked me for the name of my son's father
He asked me if by that time, I was sleeping with another man
When I was telling him the name of my son's father
He wrote that he didn't believe me because in the US
Only the mother knows who is father of her children
When he told me this, my heart was pounding and my face was
turning red
I had to be strong so I could win this case one day
Now I am going to court to tell my version
And I am going to ask for exoneration and compensation from the
state of Oregon
But no amount of money is worth my reputation

The Concha and the River Naya

At the Pacific Coast there in a corner of Colombia
There is a little town enchanted
For name, it has the Concha and is sprayed for the river Naya
The land and his colorful, I have met many places
I can say with pride that you are the only town that changes dress
Here grows the bananas, *planto*, rice, *borojo*, *piña*, y papaya
And other fruits and vegetables grow by the river Naya
Here we need the government's help to be available to produce the land
However, our government in our country never opens the map
Because he doesn't know our necessity
Here grows the poor like nature
However, we are people with nobility, and we do not put our heads down

The Day When You Leave

From the day you left, my heart was sad
The pain that you caused me with your departure hurt me
I could not forget it
But when another man came to my door and gave me an offer of love
From that moment, my life changed
I am a different person today
The love cured my heart and the years of suffering,
and one day he changed
Today I learned that when love's door closes, you do not need
to cry a lot
Another door will open for you
So don't throw away the key to your heart

The Department of Colombia

In Bojaya, a tragedy that shook Colombia
One morning in the month of May
At the church from the town
Here in a cylinder spot taking everything in his way
Children and adults killed
The government was present after the tragedy
Promising to help the town and the people
But his promise never came true
Leaving the people with the pain for losing their family
And more pain for a promise that was not kept
He forgot them and left them alone
Never to fulfill his promise

The Dog at My House

When I heard the news that you did not love the dog at my house
The dog was looking at me and laughing.
He already knew this because your look was cold
One dog smells another dog; he did not tell me before because he did
not want to cause me pain
I hope that you are valiant and have intelligence to go far away
Because I do not want to see you again even in the shadow of a mirror;
your presence bothers me
After I loved you so much, today you are out of my heart
Do not be surprised when you see another man has taken your place
I won't guard your sorrow because you did not have any value
You deserve this

The Liars

The liars from the state of Oregon took my son away from me
They did this to give him protection because I spanked him with a belt
Today the same liars are sending him to prison when he doesn't have
any money to give them for their retirement
I feel embarrassed when I see people that don't do anything about the
liars, and they are growing more than the delinquents are
They take children away from their parents
For no reason and give them to another family
When they don't have a clue to whom they are
Some of these people have a lot of problems with drugs
They only take on the children for the money

The Life

Looking at the sky I saw the stars, oh how beautiful they are
I feel forever that I want to be alive
The life is so beautiful
The secret to be alive is to smile and to have eyes to see all the beautiful
things we have in this land and in the sky
Smile when you get down; smile when you get up
Because the smile from today, tomorrow won't be the same
It doesn't matter if you smile one million times today; you won't regain
what you lost yesterday
Smiling is delicious and never makes you feel bad
Smile today and tomorrow after tomorrow, the smile will be there
because it never gets old
Wherever you go, the smile is part of your life and keeps you alive

The Love

Love is a feeling of happiness and sadness
When it came, it made us happy
And when it is leaving, you feel down
Like the wind flying down a tree, turning this on underbrush
When you find a good love, do not forget to take care of it
Because when the flowers wither, they never bloom again
Love is the same
Love is the most beautiful thing that God planted on this earth
Who can tell me that I am wrong; I can swear they were never born
Life without love is like a garden without flowers
There is no treasure in the world that can replace love

The Menopause

It is time that men start understanding
Menopause does not attack the women only
Menopause does not choose by race or religion
It attacks the hormones of the women and the men
We have to understand that when it comes
Because this can ruin marriages
Wives and husbands change their tempers
We can make this better by taking each other's hands
And remembering the love that one day we swore in front of God
Some men retire when they get old and some wives do not
Support them because they are at home
Remember when you married him and he was going to work You were
kissing him good-bye and counting the hours, waiting for him to return
When he was coming back, he did not want to eat his dinner
Because he wanted to eat with you
Today so many couples are different
There are some men that are lost and go to the streets looking for
another atmosphere
When their wives discover this, they always lie; they say that they didn't
want to find another lady and only wanted to discover if they
were impotent

The Rich

Some of the rich, with their fortune, call themselves people of royalty
They do not care if the poor go hungry and living on a lagoon
Rich who grow fortune, it is time to start helping the poor
Put your hand on your chest and touch your heart
You don't have to call a poor person to your house and open the door
Because you live thinking, the poor have an infection
And if they touch you, you will be contaminated
You can give them a hand, just open the door in your heart
Use a little money and open a charity foundation
Because poor and rich are brothers in God's eyes
It does not matter the race, skin color, or where they come from
Remember that the day when we die
The fortune stays here on land, causing family turmoil
The only thing we take with us is a coffin

The Smile

The smile is the key that opens the heart
Anyone that does not smile is locked in his own
The smile is delicious; I love to smile every moment with the
people and to myself
Those that don't know how to smile don't know what is pleasure
If you cannot smile, that is very sad because the smile is so good, and
your life without that has no reason to be alive

Two Tears in My Eyes

I won't say anything to you
But the two tears in my eyes are to say good-bye
It is hard to say good-bye when you really love somebody
It is time to say good-bye forever
Tomorrow when you wake up, I won't be in our bed
I am going to take the first train
I was tired of your lies
I gave you all my love and part of my life
And you repaid me with treachery
I wish you good luck to find somebody
And I hope you change and treat her better than me
Always remember that you were born from a woman's abdomen;
remember, the clock never stops
Think about when the sun goes down and you are lonely; it is like you
are dead but still above the ground

Where Are the Human Rights?

Mr. President Albaro Uribe
Bedroom for rent, no children allowed
House for rent, no children allowed
Apartment for rent, no children allowed
Ranch hand needed, no children allowed
Looking for secretary, must be beautiful and young
Looking for maid, white only no blacks
Help wanted, only between the ages of eighteen to twenty-five
This is what I find in the Colombian classified ads
Can anybody do something for this vulgar
Discrimination that makes my heart pound
Where is the president? Where is the law?
My blood is getting hot, and I do not like that
This is something that is not acceptable, and the president is responsible
Open your eyes. Are you smart?
Are you too busy to read the newspaper, or do you have access to that?
This is painful and it embarrasses me because people ask me if we have
a president to make the laws in our country
Please put your belt on and adjust your pants

The Yarn Dress

America, wake up with gloves on your hands
When I know Colombia has the most beautiful climate
We show our belly buttons in summer or winter
I woke up this morning wearing a dress made of yarn
When I was drinking coffee on the bottom, I saw Pastrana
I broke the porcelain cup
Because I run away from my land of Colombia
Who is going to save us? We can't trust the government
Because the head of the country and has no respect for us

Are You Happy?

How are you today? How is your new love? Tell me the truth,
are you happy or are you sad?
I want to help if you can forgive me; I will tell you that you are out
of my heart, and I will find someone to take your place and to give me
something that I lost.
He will help me to take you out of my heart
Today I love him very much and I discovered that when someone loves
you, they give everything for that person
Because the love is unconditional
I love him very much with all my heart.

Be Careful with That

Changing your life is not very easy.
That changes your hormones and changes your emotions.
Be ready for that. Do not be so unhappy because this is nobody's fault
when you feel sad. Stand and walk; when you feel hot, go and take a
bath. If you feel cold, go and sit at the porch.
Try hard not to destroy everybody life's putting you in a hole. Because
only God knows why he makes the ladies have that.
This is the menopause; it is not the end of your life.
Some ladies turn so sour, thinking that they are ready to die.
This is a part of life.

Colombian and American Pride

I am from another country looking for a better life
Do not ask me where I am from; if you will hurt my heart.
Use your brain or shut your mouth because I love my land
It is not my land's fault, a lot of corruption comes from the bad people.
They don't show the beautiful things that Colombia has; they just show
the drug problem and all the crime.
It is, as the government does not care about that.
If I were the government, that would stop
I would show the good to stop the bad because the bad things incite the
people to keep going and hear more.
Have you seen the good places and the green resort that we have?
Have you seen the good people?
There are Indians, whites, and blacks
Do you think that all the hearts are bad, or don't you think that
Colombia was made by God?

Come Down and Cry

Cry if you need to. The tears are free. Talk if you have mouth. Do not swat what you're taught. God is the only one who can stop that. Do not let anybody take this right.
God makes you live a free life. Do not make trouble to be behind bars.
The prison is bad; always think before you act and do something bad. Ask God to save you from that and everything by your side.

Don't Buy Colombian Drugs

USA has to stop supporting Colombia from producing drugs.
USA has some fault because many of the people from here buy drugs.
I do not just blame my country and say it is bad because the big money
comes from this side. Some of the Americans who do not know how that
works need to stop opening their mouths wide to talk about it, hurting
many good hearts.
Not all the people there grow drugs; this is a business from people who
think bad and don't look back to see how our country is turning bad, and
it is the government's fault not to get everyone a job before they start
taking the bad offers to go and work for whomever is making the
country rotten and worse.

Eating for Free

Eating for free does not taste good, I am sure.
When you do not like to work, you stink to the hard people that work.
When they see you at the store, paying with your food stamps and you
can't decide what you want to buy
You do not have the power to ask for something better than that in your
life, and you feel like a skunk.
That embarrasses your mom. That embarrasses your dad.
They work hard to support you and other parasites that do the
same as you do.
Everyone should have the right to stop feeding the lazy people and
make them change their life, if they do not want to die.
This is not a country where you can die from hunger because this is a
country where you can find something to do.
Live America. Live all who work.
Let all the lazy people find a place in a hole.

Find a Job

Everyone has the right to work to be alive
Do not live like a parasite waiting for someone to feed you when you
have your hands and feet.
Don't do that; move up and go find a job.
I'm not your mother, and I'm not your dad
I have a family who does not have enough to eat, not enough clothes,
and it makes me mad when I have to pay to support you.
Do you have any shame when you go to the store to spend the money
that you did not earn?
This is disgusting and is getting worse than before.
I believe you are stealing.
GO FIND A JOB!

God Is In Charge of Your Life

God is the only one in charge to decide how long everyone will live. Do not let anybody tell you when you will die and do not think to decide about somebody's life.

Take care of your life, do not use a knife, do not use a bottle; if you can run not to be hurt, try that very hard.

That can teach somebody to change their mind and cower down to the ground, asking you to pardon because it would not be a right decision to send you to the other side before God calls.

God Loves You, God Loves Us

Thank you, President Bush, for doing a good job defending the country
and keeping freedom. I will give you a million claps. This is using
your mind and having your pants on and tight. Thank you for providing
opportunity to all the good people from my country and other countries
to live here and have a better life, and thank you too. Take a look at this
land too; it does not matter where we were born because everybody is
producing and taking care of the land.
God said that this is right, and he never tried to keep the good people in
a different side.
Take care of the good people. Do not send us back to the hell we ran
away from to save ourselves.

God, Please Stop That

The animals are smarter. I hope that the bad man changes his mind
and thinks better than an animal.
To change the world and stop the wars.
This is not how God wanted to see us.
Killing people with weapons and drugs, destroying the kids.
Everybody who is behaving this bad, even in hell won't find a space.
The evils don't want that they take his space and put him away.

My Great Uncle Died

I don't remember how old I was, but one afternoon years ago, when I was a little girl, I saw a man walking with my dad, and I overheard what he was saying to my dad that my grandmother's brother died with the most terrible death that I ever thought of.
A crazy man was in love with one of his daughters; he did not like him because he was a very bad person.
He came to my great uncle's house and hit his daughter.
That relationship was not right, and the bad man took a big machete and cut him to more than one hundred pieces.
Oh my goodness, that hurt all the family and the population. That man was evil because if he committed a crime, he would pay off in jail and he would be out in the street the next day.
He committed many crimes, and everybody with him to be in hell, but he was not welcome there because he was very bad.
I grew up; many years later, I saw him in a little town where I moved.
I saw him in a wheelchair, and his finale was very bad.
I wish he found a place to go and paid for all his crimes over there.
I feel very bad for his mother and father because they were very nice people.

Do Not Hide and Lie

Do not be embarrassed to tell the truth when a man or woman hurt you.
It does not matter if they do not live abruptly.
Do not try to hide. That can cost your life. Do not tell a lie to keep
them out of the bars.
Living with the pain for life is not right.
Who hurt you one time is going to hurt you for your whole life.
I am just telling you, but this is your life and you decide.

If You Live Here, Love the Land

When I hear somebody from here or another land talking bad
about this country,
I want to shut their mouth and sometimes I do because I believe why
they are here if they do not like the country where we find food to eat.
The crazy people from here who don't like to live here need to take off
and go to another land to see what it is like to live in another land.
To see what they find and how life is—working from morning till night
to make in one day there what they make in two hours here.
My country is beautiful and has many talented, smart people, but the
problem is that you have to be almost perfect to find a job.
You can drive a taxicab after seventeen years of study with your diploma
hanging on the wall, getting dusty and old like you.

Indians, Whites, and Blacks

No to discrimination; in God's way, we are the same
It does not matter if you are tall, short, skinny or fat; handsome,
beautiful, or not.
If your eyes are blue, brown, or black, it does not change your mind; we
have the same color of blood.
Love yourself and feel proud of who you are; the most important is what
is in your heart and how you treat your life and other people
To get returns from God wherever you walk.
This is a reality; this is not a lie
If you treat yourself bad, another will walk on top of your head
If you cannot make your own life happy, what will the other ones feel?
Nobody can make your life change if you do not do your part using your
mind and your heart.
You can be rich, you can be a king; if you don't love who you are, you
will be the worst.

Injustice

I do not support injustice, and I do not break what the law said. But my heart wants to come out when I see how some people act, pardoning the people who rape other people, letting them run free in the streets to keep doing it over again. Sometimes, they pardon the killer when the crime was not to defend his or her life. But if one is Latino, someone does not, as if even living by them said their innocence; it does not matter if the crime is not to die from hunger and injustice, that is at the other side. There is one Latino behind the bars in a jail at the state because he changed his name and came back to the country, breaking the law to survive. I do not know all about his trial because I am not his lawyer. I know only what I hear about the crime. I won't say that it was right, but I have to see people that are real criminals, and they have walked by the law's side, and it's not easy to see how they tread to break the law to survive because the Bible said help yourself and God will do the other part. What do you think about it? Would you do the same to keep your family alive, or would you just put your head down and die like a parasite with all your family by your side?

I will like the American government look at what is on the other side, to the countries that really care about our life because my country and other one. We love the life and we just fight to keep this right. We are not people who want to destroy this land. We love America. We love to be free. We love and take care of the land. We work hard; we take any job when sometimes we are educated and smart.

Leaving My Parents' House

With tears in my eyes, I said good-bye to my dad and my stepmother,
my family, and my friends when I was very young to go to the city to
work and to buy clothes. We were very poor of money but
very rich in our hearts.
It was four in the morning when my father called me to take me to my
aunts. We went to the big city, and that changed my life.

The Birds Have to Fly to Be in the Sky

The birds have to fly to be in the air, flying.
Do not destroy their lives to decorate your house; just think about how you would like it if somebody does that to you.
Take a look at your life in a little place where you can't walk free and what do you see and feel in you heart, how would you like it?
If you have one bird in jail, open your heart and the door of your house to feel the gratitude.
When they go out and fly toward the direction of the sky, let them have their own lives.
Having them in a jail is not right because they have not committed any crime.

Make Up Your Mind

Why do you hold what you can't afford?
Why do you want to see what you can't pay for?
That vanity is an error,
Living like the rich in your mind when you are poor.
Live the reality and do not be in a big holt
Some people show the exterior, and they don't care if the stomach is
empty or full
If you are empty inside you, life will be sore
It does not matter if you dress well and you are covered with gold
Happiness starts from your interior
If you cover this, you are better than everything
Even a mine of gold.

Mr. President Bush

American flag: symbol of peace, liberty, and love; with your three colors—red, white, and blue—and your fifty stars, you are part of my life.

You deserve to be up and taller than our eyes. My heart pound and—pound with hapiness—when I see you at the sky. You look beautiful and amazing, but my heart pounds—and go down when I see you on the ground.

Someone has to stop treating you like a piece of garbage, putting your image on the cigarette packs to support this nasty war that is not on your side. Mr. President Bush, where are you? Please take a look and make this come true. I respect what you have done for this country and this land, but when I see this sacred symbol in the garbage or on the ground, I have a feeling to go to the White House and pull your pants down to spank you like a mom. To make you think twice and teach the cigarette companies to respect the flag.

Mr. Alvaro Uribe

I am tired of hearing that many people are hungry and mad because you
won't give them a job.
Everyone is tired of working for ridiculous pay
It is an offense to what they do
That is just for coffee and bread; it is not enough to buy decent food.
If you buy pants, you can't buy an underwear
That is one of the reasons that is turning our country bad
Because the pay keeps the stomach tight.
I talked with a mother of three children; she almost made me cry
Wearing the underwear wet because the sun could not come out or
putting the change behind the refrigerator, not to wear the same and
smell bad.
What is that? I do not know you, and I do not want to embarrass you,
but your responsibility is to give everyone the opportunity to work.
Because the constitution says that you open your mouth very wild,
talking about millions at job and giving arms to millions of Colombians
to protect their family and their lives
I saw you on the television, and I said that is blah-blah-blah because I
already had to live with the other liars before you who treated me like a
criminal to produce my food.

My Father God

Who does not believe in God, that is very bad. He who does not believe
does not respect his mom or dad. God is real. God is love. He created
the good things; he did not create the bad.
God is with me when I wake up. I love you, God. You are my boss.
I would not do anything without your permission because you are the
owner of my life and my heart. Please protect my family, my friends,
and my neighbors and watch everybody over the land. Put your hands in
front of everyone who wants to do destruction in the world.

My Life Is Divided

I am Colombian and American
Colombia saw me born and grew up, and America adopted me
like my mom and dad.
Here I found another life different from my natural land.
There are not a lot of festivals and parties here like in my country
Here you live comfortably because you'll find opportunities for
anyone—blacks, whites, or Indians.
If you like to work, then you can.
Here the job is not a crime like in my country and the other ones.
I live here very comfortably and out of headaches and pains in my butt.
Because the one that doesn't work here is lazy;
Here, there is not much discrimination if you come with the right
of emigration.
I believe that here you don't see the discrimination that I saw in my
own nation;
The people publish that in the newspaper, on the radio,
and on the television.
The human rights are over because there we don't have a
government that is intelligent;
Sometimes I think that they are more worthless than a delinquent.

Never Hurt the Love

When you have a love, you must take care of that love because another
man or woman can steal them away
Taking care of your love is good, not bad.
Do not live in your place fighting like dogs and cats
Fight with your strength coming from your heart, and use your mind, do
not kill the love.
When you kill the love, you can't bring it back to life.
If you have a love, do not hurt his or her life; it is very hard to see
someone taking your place and living there.
If you take it away, it will never come back
Because the cut is forever there.
The years can pass and you can grow old, but when the love is hurt
nothing can heal it!
Just another love.

Only Me

How difficult it is to live in a little town in a different country where you
are the only one who is different;
It is difficult when you don't understand and when you can't
speak the language.
Oh my goodness, this is hard especially when you are a social, friendly,
and happy person who loves to talk
If you do not understand the language, you just keep your mouth shut.
This is touchier. This is more than leaving your country, your family,
your habits, and many friends behind; and you are in this situation, you
cannot stop crying; it doesn't matter how strong you are.
I lived this experience and that was bad
I don't want to live my life quiet sour and sad.

Pepito Is in Our Lives

Pepito is our little dog,
He does not know how to talk, but he talks with his eyes and he knows
how to bark.
Pepito is beautiful and he takes care of us
Pepito is our hero.
He fought for his life when he was still a baby
When we went to the country to go fishing, he saved our lives
A bad rattlesnake bit his leg
He went to the doctor and spent the night there
Pepito survived.
Pepito is very special, and he makes our life very happy
Pepito, we love you
You are part of our life.

Respect Your Job

If you have a dog or cat in your house, I am sure you love them very
much, and God bless you for doing that and for being loving and patient
to those that can't talk.
Do not bring hairs of your pet to your job
Because that is telling the people that you did not take a bath.
Come to work clean. Help the business grow.

Saturday Nightmare

In 1992, my daughter and I were kidnapped by the military
for two hours.
On a Saturday morning, my daughter and I were coming from a town
where the barge from Zaragoza, Antioquia, is one hour away.
We were traveling for half an hour, and the military stopped the bus to
do a revision and to see our documentation; everyone over the age of
eighteen had to keep an identification card to travel.
It did not matter how far you were going; it was the rule.
They told everybody to get off the bus, and everyone did.
When they were doing the revision, they asked questions about a
civic stop;
We were telling them that we did not know anything because that was
the truth, and if someone knew, they were not going to tell anything
because no one wanted to die.
This was a place where anyone who opened their mouth to take any side
was called a *sapo* by the military or by the guerrilla and was not going
to live much longer;
When the military asked for information about the guerrillas, I told
them that I didn't know anything, and I couldn't tell them that my
daughter and I were going to Zaragoza to work by selling food.
Ten minutes after they stopped the bus, there was a shot from the hills.
The military made us get under the bus, and they started shooting back
toward the mountain using the bus as cover.
Everyone was screaming and praying to God and the images that we
believe in to save us and not let us die.
I remember that I put a suitcase on top of my daughter's head, and I lay
on top of her to protect her from the bullets;
Then after four or five minutes, the shooting stopped and the military
made us get up and kept asking questions where the guerrillas were, and
we said we don't know anything.

They told us to get on the bus, and just as we were getting on the bus, a shot came from the hills again, and they started shooting back, and this time we were thinking we were not going to survive.

You didn't want to be there after the second attack stopped, so the military let the bus go and everyone was shaking, but my daughter was stronger than everyone else because she didn't know what was going on.

When the bus got into town, I said to God, thank you for giving me another opportunity to live, and I promised him from that day forward, I would be a new person.

When my daughter and I got up from our seats and I took my suitcase and my groceries, there was one soldier coming into the bus and everyone was curious because if the guerrillas were attacking the military, why was he coming by himself?

When he saw me coming to the doorstep and the driver knew that it was my stop, the soldier asked me, where are you going?

I responded to my house and he said no, you have to come with me to the base to see my commander.

I started crying and everyone was afraid, but no one said anything; he made me get off with my daughter who was only ten years old at the third stop, in front of the police, and talked on his radio to the commander.

He told him that they got one of the guerrillas

Then the policeman told me to go and to leave my suitcase there because he knew what my job was;

We walked two blocks to the bus station.

Everyone there was asking me what was going on, and I told them I did not know, but if something happens to my daughter and me, the military was responsible.

By this time, I already had a headache and a fever

The soldier asked the bus driver to take us to the base; it was about a mile away from there;

I was very nervous because this was a crazy mistake.

When we got to the base, we got off, and he paid the driver; we had to walk a little way to get to the base

I was walking and holding on to my daughter's hand
When we got to the base, the commander was waving at me and saying
hello, *muchachita*—this was a nickname for the woman guerrillas.
He asked, do you have anything to tell me about your partners
I told him I have no partners and I don't know what I am doing here
with my daughter.
At that moment, the soldier told his commander that when the shooting
started, I was yelling why are you guys doing this now, I am here now
and I am one of you.
When he told this lie, I had a bad feeling; I was thinking to myself, If
my daughter wasn't here and I didn't have children, I would jump at him
and take his rifle and shoot him.
I told the commander that this man is a liar, and he was telling a
terrible lie.
Fifteen minutes later, I saw somebody that I knew came up to us,
wearing a military uniform, to say "hello, España, how are you, and he
said hello to my daughter and said you are growing up so fast and you
are getting very beautiful.
He asked me what are you doing here, and I told him what was
going on;
He told the commander that this was not right and asked his commander
to let me go.
He said he could vouch for me
She is an honest and hardworking woman, and I know that she came to
this and we are friends;
She is not a guerrilla.
He was a top secret worker for the military for many years; after he
finished his mission, he went back to wear the uniform.
After he told the commander to let me go, I thanked him for telling the
truth, and he walked us back to the bus and we went back to pick up my
suitcase from the police command, and everyone was asking me what
was going on and that people around town had heard that the military
had arrested two guerrillas.
They did not know that the unlucky person that day was me because
they said it was a man and a woman.

My friends didn't have any idea because I was only a food seller, and now God had saved me from people like that and saved all the people who are innocent and from lies like that, who have to pay for something they never did.

When I got to my house, I was very sick but I decided to cook and put everything together to work that night;

Many people were telling me to leave that town after what happened. Because it can be dangerous when somebody blame you for something of that magnitude;

But I said I am not hiding anything and I do not have to leave.

When I was cooking the eggs, about twelve soldiers who talked to the commander passed by the house where I was living, and that was the end of this Saturday nightmare.

Later, we discovered that it was the military doing this to get information on the guerrillas from us.

Silicone Ladies

Oh, my goodness, what is that?
Why are some women going around with a lot of vanity?
They get surgery in their breast, surgery in their stomachs,
and surgery in their butts.
There is almost nothing that you cannot see.
This is disgusting, crazy to believe; they put their lives in danger, and
sometimes they stop eating to lose weight when the poor are starving
because they have no money.
They sacrifice, saving and cutting expenses only for vanity.
God made the body with love and devotion.
But today you just see reconstruction.
Many have lost the money and the illusion of trying to be beautiful in
the outside and having a rotten inside and finished their life in
an intervention.
This is a disaster; they have lost their values.
You can't be happy or be beautiful if you do not make your mind look
like your interior—because what's inside gets out.
You have the control of your mind and body more than your surgeon.
You are your own doctor.

Smiling Doesn't Hurt

Smiling does not hurt or damage the heart;
What damages is the sour, and it makes you get wrinkles
like an accordion.
Do not be afraid to live life,
Do not try to smile or be happy; just do it.
Do not make your life hard; that will hurt your own heart;
It does not matter if you have problems, do not let them put you down.
I tell you this because I have an experience,
Just find the solution using your intelligence because if you are stuck,
they can lead you to dementia
The smile can make you feel good and healthy.
They who live their life happy and sour; you have to think that they are
not good, just walk by because that person does not respect his own self
and does not know how to love.

Take Care of Your Own

Before you spit in the air, think that it comes back to your face. Do not talk bad about another person when there is no reason for that because that is the same as spitting. It is like a punishment; you pay for that. Do not open your mouth so wide to talk about your neighbor's kids when you do not know if yours are doing worse.

Talented and Intelligent

I am a Colombian with pride and honor
I am talented and intelligent
I would like to be a president.
When I see the injustice in those who act demented
And who don't use their intelligence to finish with the violence
Who are destroying our country and getting worse, and they keep
on lying.
The newspaper and TV, they put aside peace at the corner
And the people keep dying from mines, cold, hunger, no medicine,
and crime.
Today, it is a crime to see and hear because the bad people and killers do
not want to leave the evidence
After they commit a crime, they clean everything on their way
To be free to commit more crimes
They are nasty, and they are dirty
They really do not care if their veins run the same blood with the person
that they kill because they are afraid of being discovered.
They can hurt their own parents
I am tired of the violence
I am going to shout loud.
Looking to the sky, Leave COLOMBIA!
The whole world, all the good people, the love, and the liberty
Say no to the lie, say no to the promise of those who has a big history or
who has come from a branch that had governed the country because if
his father was corrupted, his son will be evicted
I don't have a lot of school or a master's degree, but I have good vision
and intelligence to do a better job than many who have doctorates
I can show them that the studies and the diplomas that they won at the
best university
If I asked them only one question, I would leave them embarrassed.

The Real Life

Life is not a dream
Life is a reality
Wake up and be joyful with what you have.
It is not the time to dream; make everything real and stop dreaming
because there is no time to dream,
Just stay up and make everything come right because just to dream
takes some time to start.
Dreaming is not the way to spend your life,
If you have money or not, just think that God is on top and is the only
one who can stop you.
Believe that you own your own life and only God can decide
what will be,
God is on your side, and no one can take your family and your life.

The Workers and the Boss

You do not have to love your workers
You do not have to love your boss
But the relationship has to be good on both sides
Always remember who is putting money in the pocket
To show your workers who is the boss, you don't need to humiliate them
and treat them bad
The smart workers understand the message and do good job
The lazy won't get that; it doesn't matter if you try hard; they will give
you the finger behind your back
Here is just one solution with people like that
Write them a check and send them to look for another job because
you're not their mother or their father, and you can't spank their butts
Having unhappy people doing the job is not good and is bad luck for
your business and your pocket
If you don't like your job or you don't like the pay, go back to school to
find another way and get a job to do what you like, or just live with it;
don't cry and complain—that is what you deserve
Be happy and be tight because you do not want to use your mind and
that will be your life.

This Land Is Yours and Mine

How painful it is to see your children crying for food when you
do not have money or a job
This is painful and sad
These hurts sometimes hurt your mind
These sometimes hurt you in your heart when you are looking for a job
and the line is two blocks long and it is the only job
What is sad when you go in and people look at your hair, your feet, and
your butt, and then they ask you if you have experience when you never
had a job before, and you just finished school after many sacrifices from
your mom and dad
What is sad is to go home and wait for a call that never comes
This is the reality of our country and the other ones
What is painful is to pack your clothes and leave your family, your
country, your friends, and everything you have
But with hopes of coming back with better luck
What is sad is when those dreams don't come true and some people
never come back; death surprises them before they step in another land,
and some of the family never hears from their father, mother, grandpa,
or grandma
No more violence, no more bad luck.
With the hands of God, one day everything will be turned down Poor,
rich, and magnets will be the same, stinking and rotting in their coffins.

To My Aunt

Aunt Leticia gave my sisters and me a lot of love. She helped my dad to
bring us up. Today I tell you, I love you and you are forever in my heart.
You were the most beautiful aunt that I ever had. You taught me how
to work and not to work slow when you have to do that. And made me
move away those who are in your way, losing time and talking bad about
the hard job. Thank you, Aunt. You were a very hard worker; every time
I have some work to do, I think of my father and you. The time and the
years passed, and I remember you more and more. You taught me to do
a good job, to pick fruit, and eat enough. I am sure that the good people
like you are living with the angels.
Live with the Virgin Mary and God.
Live together with my father, my mother, and my stepmother, and all our
family who are already at the sky.
My grandparents, uncles, aunts, and any other family.

To My Brothers and Sisters

To all my brothers and sisters, I say hello with my heart; I love you wherever you are. It does not matter the distance; the love is enough to cut thorough that. It is sad when one year passes and another comes up. But the real love never stops growing.

I love you, sister Dilia. I love you, sister Flor. I love you, Sorlenny. We grew up together, and that was the best life when we used to sit down together, side by side.

I love you, sister Eduicia. I love you, brother Asimion. I love you, brother Camilo. I love you, brother Sebastian. Please tell me where you are. I love you, brother Calisto. I love you, brother Pedro Juan. Let me know if you are at the land or you are with our mom.

To My Father with Love

Father, who moved to the sky, I miss you very much. From when you left, my life changed and I left our country. I found a good husband who is a very good man; we have two kids, and I named one after you, Dad; and every day, that brings joy to my life when I call them and say your name, it's very nice. I have never forgotten you, Father. I have never forgotten everything that you taught me. It is like a tape measure and I am trying to transmit that to my kids, but the love is very different in the new generation, and sometimes the kids call the parents old-fashioned when you are trying to teach them traditions from Lincoln City, Oregon.

I write this memory for you with all my heart and love.

My husband and my kids say hello.

ThankYou to All Our Workers

Thank you to all the good people who can get along and work for us;
Thank you to all the other ones could not go alone.
Thank you to live away from my side;
Thank you to all my workers that give me their hand, working in the
cold and in the heat.
Thank you to everyone that gives me their support to not close the doors
when it is snowing or when there is ice on the ground;
Thank you to all of them who do their jobs with dedication and love and
not just thinking when is the next paycheck coming.
Thank you for all of them who do the job with respect and
good attitude;
Thank you for those that have good ideas for us to help the
business grow.
Thank you to all who know that taking care of the business is taking
care of their own job.

God Sent Me Two Angels to Save My Life

I was walking at five thirty in the morning to the bus stop on my
way to work
When I was walking by a football field, a man came from there; I was
walking fast, and he started talking loud to me,
He was asking me for an address.
I was about three blocks away from the bus stop, and the neighborhood
was sleeping because it was Easter.
I was very nervous because I was six months pregnant with
my daughter.
I passed by a friend's house, but he was so close to me I did not have
time to stop and knock and ask for help,
He kept on walking fast, and when I was two blocks from the bus stop,
I saw two people over there, and I started running like an athlete to look
for help.
When I was almost there, he told me, look what I have, and I kept
running, but I looked back and saw he was carrying a big shiny knife.
I was not carrying anything because the stupid law does not allow the
good people to carry anything to defend ourselves and our families.
God saved me, and he sent me two angels at the bus stop
They took care of me until the bus came, as they were waiting for the
same bus.
If the angels were not at the parking lot, I did not know what I would
have done because the problem with violence is big;
If you knock on a door for help, the people do not know if it is true or if
it is somebody trying to go in the house to hurt them.
This is a sad reality that is getting worse every day, and nobody is able
to fix it because the corruption is on top of the same law.

You are My Life

to my four children

God gave me four beautiful children for a present,
I have them in my heart day and night,
They are my life.
It does not matter if they are perfect,
It does not matter if they are far away.
They are always with me in my heart
Sometimes I smile for them and sometimes I cry,
This is part of being a mother and is a part of life.
The love of a mother is the most sacred because that is a
love conspirator.
The love of a mother is sacred, and no one can put that away;
The love of my children is the most beautiful that God sent to me.
When I see my children leave, I feel a response; my heart pounds and
pounds when they leave, and my heart pounds when they are coming,
but this time, it pounds with happiness and is easy to stop

Your In-laws Are in Your Life

How can you love the fruit if you do not love the tree?
How can you love your husband or wife if you do not love the persons
who brought them to life?
The relationship has to start with your husband's or your wife's mom
and dad, or your marriage will be bad.
It does not matter if they like you;
You are the person that is taking what they planted.
You have to teach them how to love to make them give it in return
They can be like a stick, but you can make them throw that back
and be soft;
When they see that you really care about them by showing
respect and love.
Don't put your children in between to try to hurt them with that because
they love the grandkids more than you think;
Putting them in between is like giving them a shot and destroying
your kids' life.